FIVE
5 FINGER
PIANO

3RD EDITION

 CARTOON FUN

ISBN 978-1-5400-3095-5

Visit Hal Leonard Online at
www.halleonard.com

Contact Us:
Hal Leonard
7777 West Bluemound Road
Milwaukee, WI 53213
Email: info@halleonard.com

In Europe contact:
Hal Leonard Europe Limited
42 Wigmore Street
Marylebone, London, W1U 2RN
Email: info@halleonardeurope.com

In Australia contact:
Hal Leonard Australia Pty. Ltd.
4 Lentara Court
Cheltenham, Victorla, 3192 Australia
Email: info@halleonard.com.au

Bob the Builder
(Main Title)

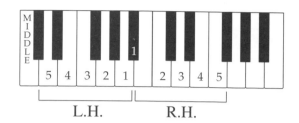

Words and Music by
Paul K. Joyce

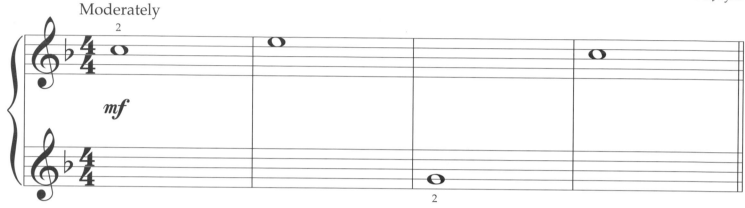

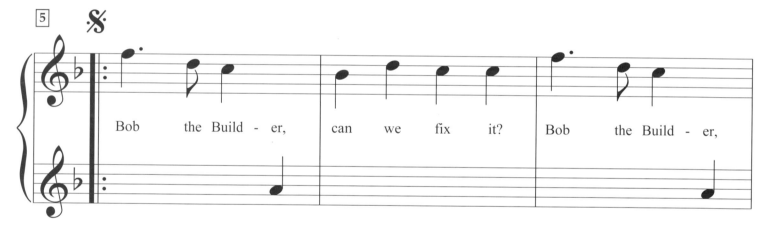

Bob   the Build - er,   can we   fix   it?   Bob   the Build - er,

Duet Part (Student plays one octave higher than written.)
Moderately

Linus and Lucy
from A CHARLIE BROWN CHRISTMAS

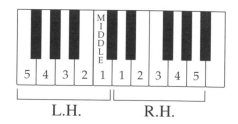

By Vince Guaraldi

Moderately

Duet Part (Student plays one octave higher than written.)

Moderately

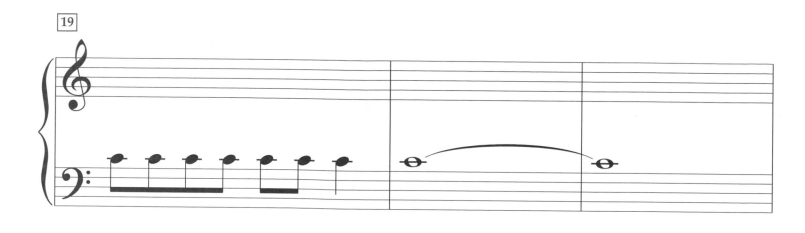

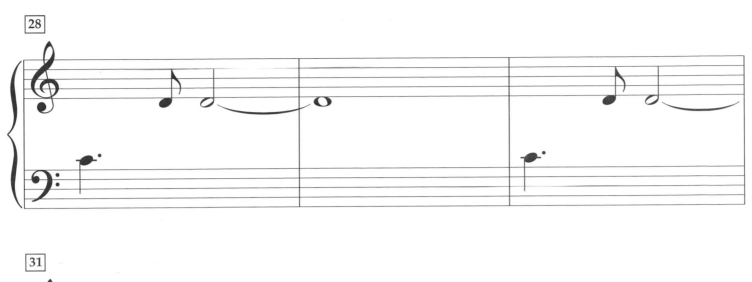

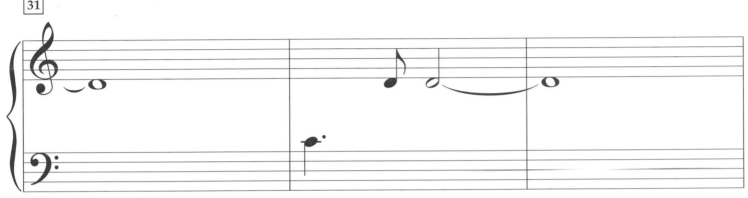

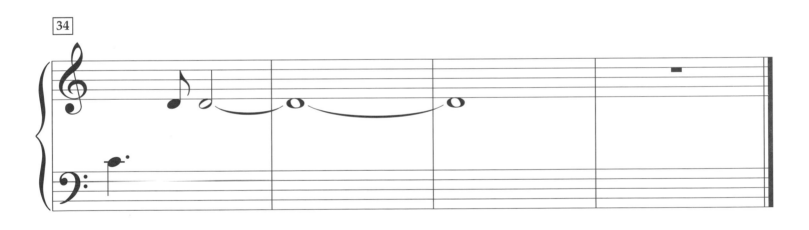

9

PAW Patrol Theme

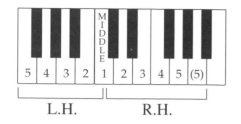

L.H. R.H.

Words and Music by Jeff Cohen,
Molly Kaye, Scott Krippayne
and Michael "Smidi" Smith

Moderately fast

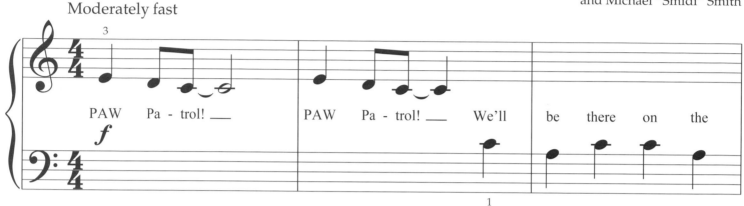

PAW Pa - trol! ___ PAW Pa - trol! ___ We'll be there on the

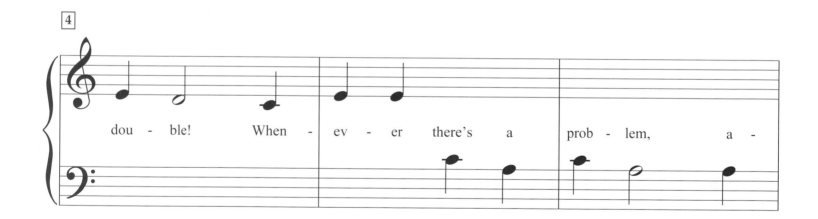

dou - ble! When - ev - er there's a prob - lem, a -

Duet Part (Student plays one octave higher than written.)

Moderately fast

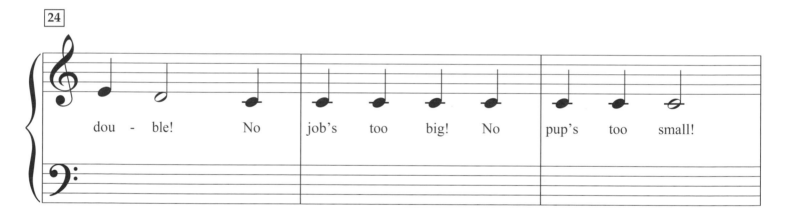

Pokémon Theme
Theme to the English adapted anime series POKÉMON

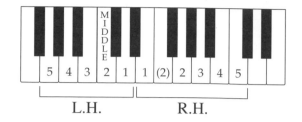

L.H.   R.H.

Words and Music by T. Loeffler
and J. Siegler

Moderately fast

mf   I wan-na be the   ver - y best, like   no one ev- er was. _

To catch them is   my real test, to

Duet Part (Student plays one octave higher than written.)

Moderately fast

15

Got - ta catch 'em all! A heart __ so true. __ Our cour - age will

pull us through. You teach me and I'll teach you. Po - ké - mon! __

__ Got - ta catch 'em all, got - ta catch 'em all! __ Po - ké - mon!

Theme from Spider Man

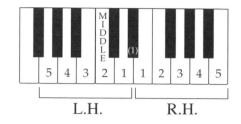

L.H.   R.H.

Written by Bob Harris and
Paul Francis Webster

Fast

mf Spi - der Man,   Spi - der Man,   does what - ev - er a
Is he strong?   Lis - ten, bud;   he's got ra - di - o -

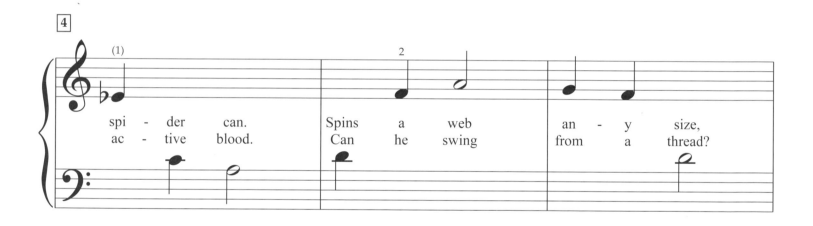

spi - der can.   Spins a web   an - y size,
ac - tive blood.   Can he web swing   from a thread?

Duet Part (Student plays two octaves higher than written.)

Fast

mp

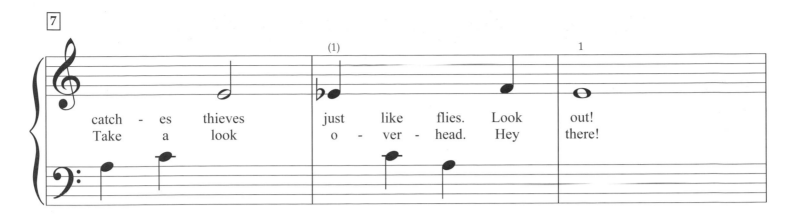

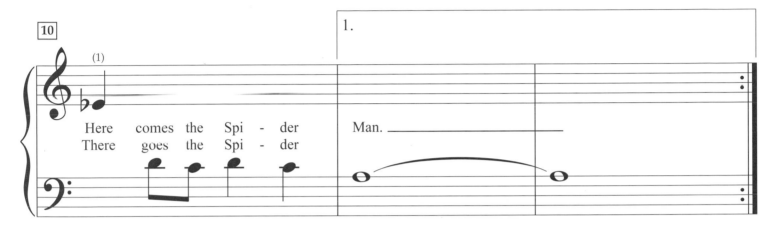

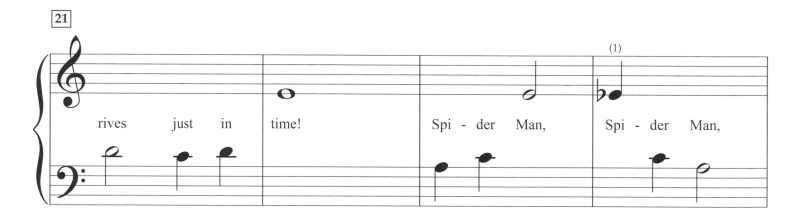

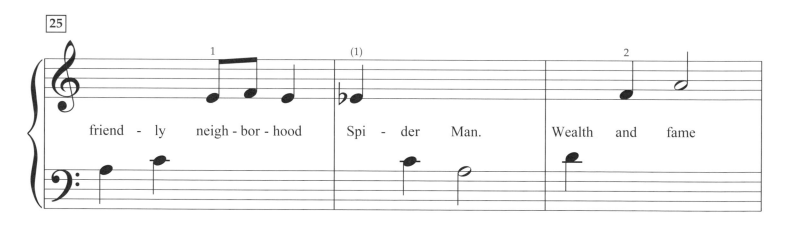

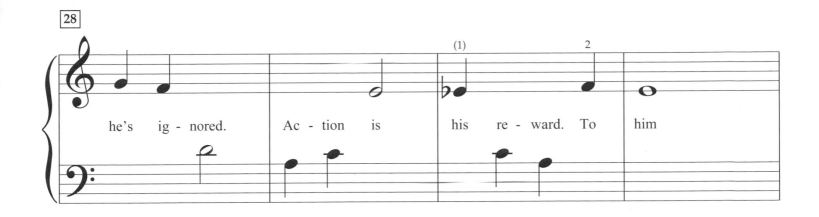

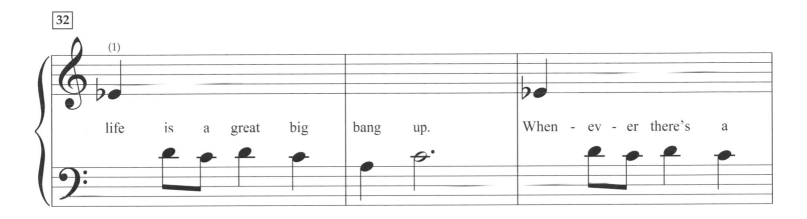

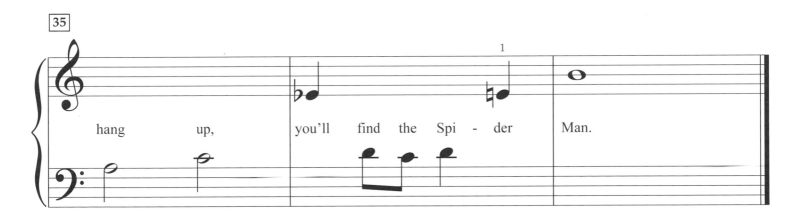

SpongeBob SquarePants
Theme Song
from SPONGEBOB SQUAREPANTS

Words and Music by Mark Harrison,
Blaise Smith, Steve Hillenburg
and Derek Drymon

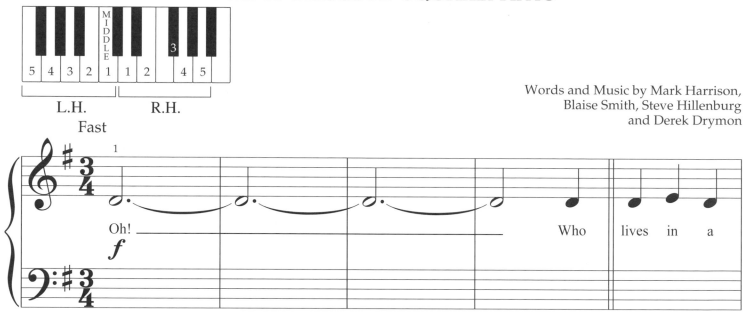

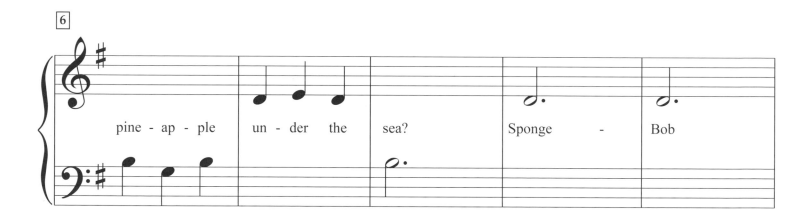

Duet Part (Student plays one octave higher than written.)

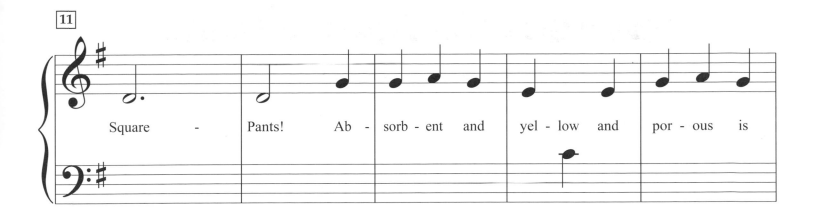

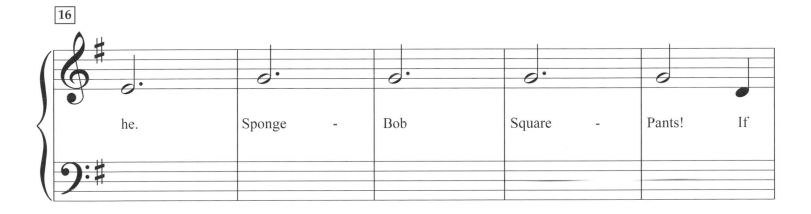

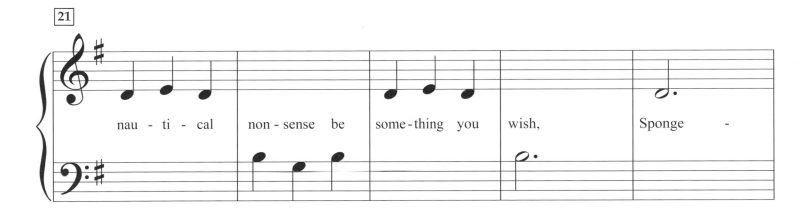

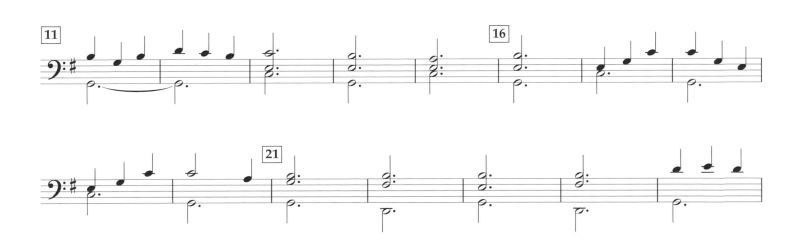

Bob Square - Pants! Then drop on the deck and

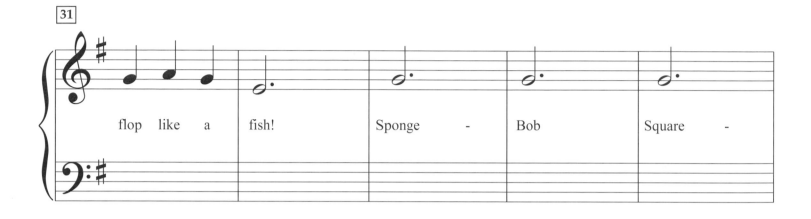

flop like a fish! Sponge - Bob Square -

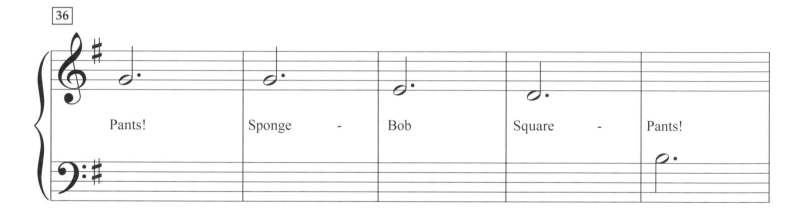

Pants! Sponge - Bob Square - Pants!

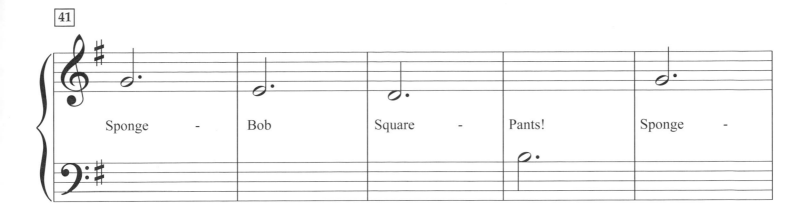

Sponge - Bob Square - Pants! Sponge -

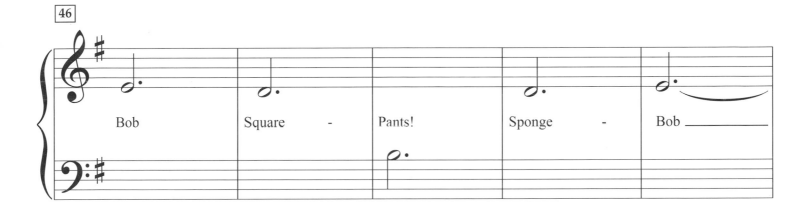

Bob Square - Pants! Sponge - Bob _____

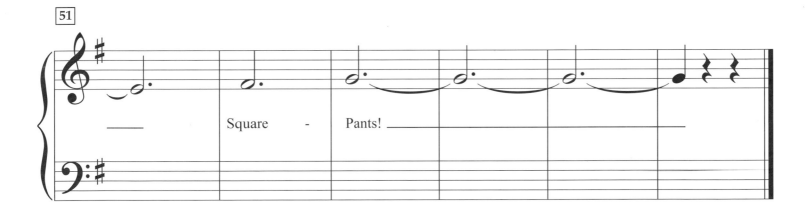

_____ Square - Pants! _____

Thomas the Tank Engine

(Main Title)
from THOMAS THE TANK ENGINE

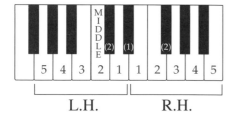

L.H. R.H.

Words and Music by
Ed Welch

With a bounce

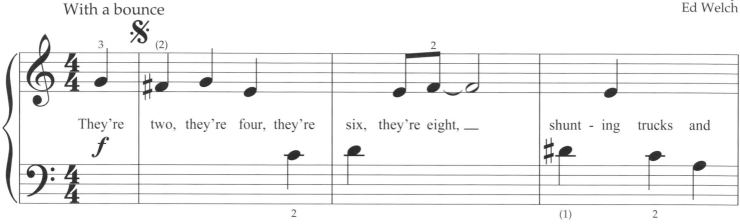

They're two, they're four, they're six, they're eight, — shunt - ing trucks and

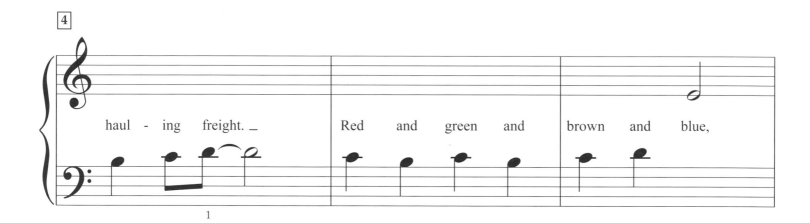

haul - ing freight. — Red and green and brown and blue,

Duet Part (Student plays one octave higher than written.)

With a bounce

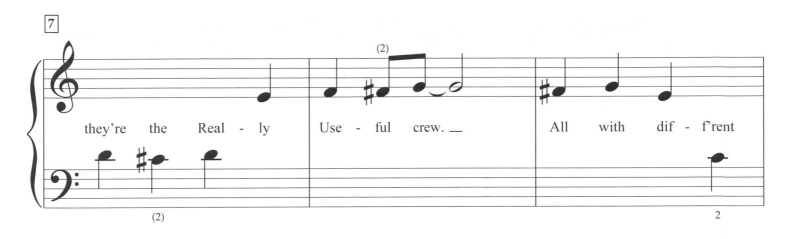

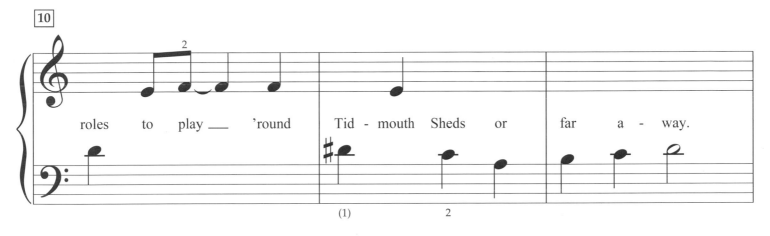

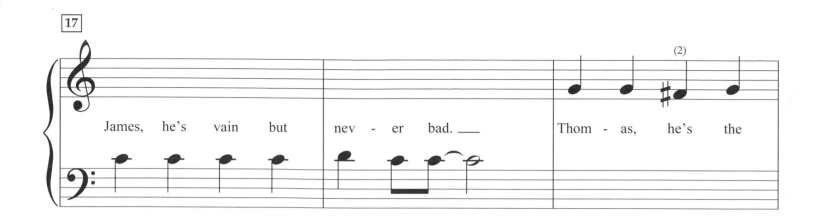

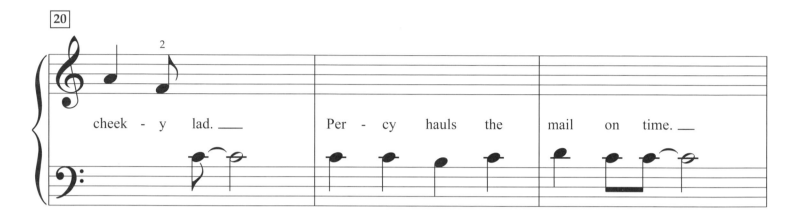

26 knows her stuff. ___ Hen - ry toots and huffs and puffs.

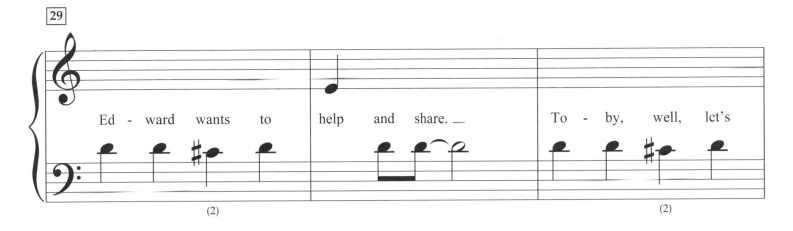

29 Ed - ward wants to help and share. ___ To - by, well, let's

(2)   (2)

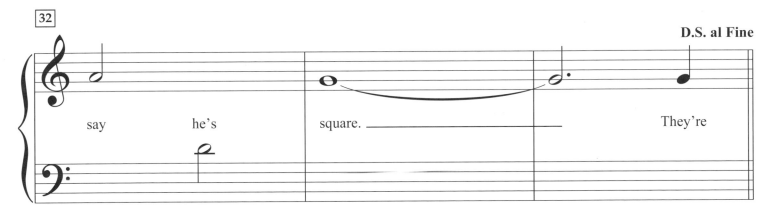

D.S. al Fine

32 say he's square. _____ They're

26   29

32   **D.S. al Fine**

Wallace and Gromit Theme
from WALLACE AND GROMIT

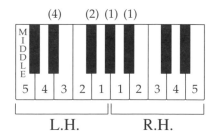

By Julian Nott

March tempo

Duet Part (Student plays one octave higher than written.)

March tempo

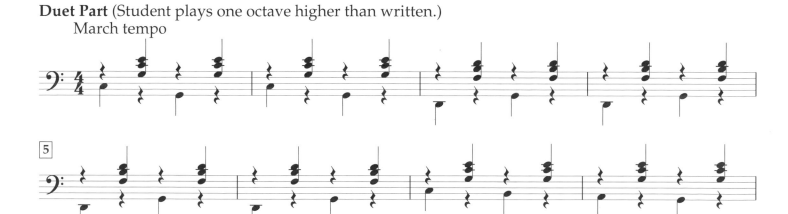